UPSTAIRS

Book of poetry and prose

Marina Sergeyeva

Leo Publishing, LLC

This is a work of fiction. All characters and events portrayed in the short stories are either fictitious or are used fictitiously.

UPSTAIRS

Cover art: Marina S. Buryak
www.marinasergeyeva.webs.com

This book is printed on acid-free paper.

Leo Publishing, LLC
St. Augustine, FL
www.leopublishing.net

Library of Congress Control Number: 2011928937

ISBN: 978-0-9834735-1-0

Printed in USA

Lord, I'm honored that my hands and sense you *guide* **D**

And, Mom, you planted and nourished the talents *provided* in *m* **E**

Dad (Chris), thanks for hearing the poems I to *thee recite* **D**

Sabrina's inspiration burst my creativity into *excited confett* **I**

Grandma seeks heart, truth, love in what she hears, like a *libretti criti* **C**

Grandpa was always and still is my *fanatic magm* **A**

My family in Ukraine cares and gives prayers despite the move that I and *ma go* **T**

My dear mentors and teachers, some kids are uneducated but, thanks to you, *not* **I**

Of course, friends and fans, I'm grateful that my work you can relate or *try s* **O**

Special and last, the angel of my father, I appreciate your constant *co*-protectio **N**

Leo Publishing is proud to introduce a young girl, born abroad and in command of another language, who arrived to America without missing a beat of creativity in her transformation of writing and poetic skills from Russian and Ukrainian languages to English. Marina has created an innovative and unique style of poetry that embodies the beauty of the written word with the perfection and symmetry of a precise mathematical formula. Her short stories are unpredictable and will lead the reader down unsuspected pathways. Marina Buryak (writing under the pen name of **Marina Sergeyeva)** is a prodigy of both literary creativity and scientific discipline. Marina graduated high school and two years of college simultaneously. After this achievement, she went on to obtain university degrees in biochemistry and mathematics with a future goal of becoming a neurosurgeon. Her first short story was published in the ***Authors of Tomorrow***, and she was awarded scholarship funding for one of her essays. With her first collection of poetry and short stories, ***Upstairs***, Marina is poised to enter the world of literature. For all that she has already accomplished, we salute her and await for her many additional works, including her book for children. Please welcome **Marina Sergeyeva.**

~Leo Publishing, LLC

(www.leopublishing.net)

A Letter to the reader,

"Spare the skins and give us the good stuff!" Introductions are boring, so I cross my digits in hopes that curiosity guided you to peek at my address to you. Thus, I invite you to read further to get acquainted with me and this book, as in it, I leap through the poetic stages of my development.

With trepidation and reserve, I can guess the places where people have free-time for books. Thus, the shorter the passage, the more likely it will be read first. Perhaps, this is not your first stop in this book. Nevertheless, I hope that the quality of the reading will allow you to graduate this book from the powder room to the sofa and maybe eventually late night reading. I write with a modern classic style, so would it be nice if we all had an electrical fireplace and some relaxation time to devote to ourselves? Reading this book, challenge yourself to find the hidden rhymes, meanings, and play-on-words, but also simply appreciate the beauty of your surroundings. With my poetry's unique forms, I intended to animate fresh interest to the cherished classical style. What marks the end of my child's section is the shift toward analytics, but don't let that be a barrier for relaxed reading. Alike, my essays have an underlying layer of meaning. I hope it is fun, though. And yes, most of my ideas were intentional. They unrolled with ease but much planning. For now, I'll look forward to the possibility of us crossing paths someday.

~Sincerely, with all my love to my readers,

Marina.

Table of Shorts

Early Childhood

Scarlet liquid

I sat in misery glaring at the scarlet liquid steaming in front of me. It was starting to haunt my thoughts by the second hour (and I am not exaggerating) of my torture. My eyes gathered streams of sorrow, yet I tried to keep happy thoughts within reach. But, how could I hold on to pleasant feelings with *that* sitting in front of me? I was alone and starting to get frustrated: frustration with a coat of boredom and pity. I looked up with a miserable look in my eyes and saw that my mom had entered the room, quietly. She knew how hard it was for me, and it was hard for her to watch. I could tell by the change in her facial expression that she saw my pitiful glance. Her features turned soft, and her stance relaxed. She looked pleasant; over there, in that light, motionless, she looked heroic and reminded me of an Italian super-model. At that moment realizing that I wasn't doing well, my wits urged me toward the right but strenuous decision.

I dug into my borshch[1] after whirling it with a spoon for the past hour. The least I could do is drink a portion and perhaps try to increase my rate of its consumption. I was always a picky eater: picky and slow. I possessed discriminating taste buds and would literally separate parts of a meal and remove items that I did not enjoy. I was always

---

[1] A Ukrainian traditional first-course meal in a form of a beet soup.

glad to have fresh vegetables or a second course of kasha, but I believed that some vegetables were far better off left alone and uncooked. Once, my mom even tried a "family game," interpretation to the "glad game" in the story of *Pollyanna*. She would give me a spoon of soup to eat for each family member's health, and I never knew that I had so many relatives! I played along not to disappoint my "relatives," but I was really eating for Mom. Besides, we didn't have a dog, so that food had to go somewhere. We didn't have any large indoor plants, either, and deceiving mamachky[2] didn't sound like a good idea anyway. If we did grow plants, I would have a hard time explaining why our plants suddenly turned red, and I'm not sure that borshch makes a good fertilizer. This kind of situation reminded me of an anecdote about a boy throwing his second course, kasha, from window of an apartment building. The ending's mood arrangement becomes apparent: Kasha lands on the head of a policeman...everyone always finds out. The last contemplation made me chuckle as I joined reality. Borshch is a tradition, which began in Ukraine, and I just have to deal with it since, I thought, I would never change my taste...

...Mmmm, the smell of dinner is overpowering my senses. Hunger took possession of me during preparation of my dinner plate... I sit here enjoying one of my favorite bowls of hot, liquid borshch!

---

[2] My Russian version of a pet name for my mom.

An old figure

Through the mist-shaded window, which reveals a mystic universe with foggy shadows, I saw an old figure gently taking form. Her shape slowly emerged upon my sight. A shadow glided from beneath her to form a pool of onyx oil prevailing over the ground. The figure's knurled body swayed slightly in the wind. I could see her hand, reaching out with an aged grace as she spotted me, waving her long, thin arms in my direction. Her slender limbs looked out of proportion to her thick body, and freely moving fingers had gentleness to them as they absorbed smiles of the sun now piercing the fog. However, *she* did not smile. Her brown eyes followed me with intensity and depth and were the darkest thing on her body. Her carelessly tangled mane was as free as the birds, which would feel comfort in her presence. Her tresses spread apart wide, covering half her body—almost entrapping her. The heat was smothering, and when I opened the window, an overpowering aroma greeted my senses. Because she acquired a new perfume, the scent seemed foreign on her. It was something fresh like the scent of April and was seducing my mind from studies to thoughts of walking barefoot in tall, crisp grass. I wanted to climb out of my window to experience the reverie. The fragrance mixed with the hovering dance of the flowers' whiff.

I noticed a talisman clasped between her extremities. This blithe sound-box softly carried a melody with the tone of a flute. If I were to ever kiss the old stranger, my lips would perceive her aridness. She manifested coarseness too rough for lips to caress. Even when I hugged her, she serrated against my skin. Her complexion developed with the mantle of years, and anyone could see that her crust made waves across her body as grooves, channels, and waterfalls. Too late I realized that I would miss her great wisdom if she was taken away from me. Her strength and freedom are contagious. I caught this fever and will have it long after she is gone.

Today strangers will appear, armed with the tools of carnage. They will seize her out of the garden....my shade, my green vault across heaven, the supplier of my very breath from her oxygen.... my beautiful tree.

Calling for love

There was trouble up ahead...A bird circled the field, looking for a meal. She spread her wings in the freedom of life. The light of the setting sun struck the bird's wings, displaying a medley of beautiful colors arranged like a rainbow, as the bird arose from the shadows. It was very rare of that kind to show up in a place like this. She needed food before night befallen. A gathering of bushes ahead showed promise. Where there is a bush, there is usually a good bug or two to be found. And so it was; right near the bush is where she spotted him, so cleverly disguised in the brown cloak of the shade.

Two rare creatures had found each other! Trying to live his life, the cricket moved quietly along his path when a sudden instinctual fear overcame him. A fight for survival would soon begin. The distance between the bell cricket and the predator shrunk with fearful swiftness. There was nothing left to do but attempt to hide in self-defense. The hunter's sharpness was better than expected; even in the near darkness with the chestnut color of the cricket, she could still see him. She was upon him now and suddenly made a sharp movement. It was at the very last second—less than a heartbeat—that it looked as if she had gotten the cricket, for he was gone.

The cricket luckily went deeper into the foliage that moment. The bird's beak pecked closer to the insect. He had to move again to another spot so that he would not turn out to be dinner for the feathered carnivore. Once, the beak was so close, his carapace felt the slight pressure as the sharp maw just missed him. After that hopeless effort, the bird finally flew away unsatisfied. If the cricket had any conscious thought, it would have been one of relief. Little did he known that this rainbow did not come after the rain but before it.

He emerged from hiding, spotting some brightly colored lights ahead. All of the lights struck the bushes and circled around the park. What a wonder! The cricket was hypnotically attracted to them even though they slightly resembled the bird that had chased him earlier. The heat being emitted didn't bother the bell cricket because he was pleasantly insulated. He was still unseen and hidden in a dark cushion of leaves. This characteristic, to never be much visible, was implanted into his instinct. That is why his shell captured the blues and the reds—cool and warm: to better blend with his surroundings. Crickets don't have much else in the way of self defense. In search of some food next, the cricket stretched out his legs and gracefully leaped deeper inward and away from the lights. He almost slipped because one of the leaves was moist from the earlier rain. He was stuck and caught upside down and everything curled around him, in a way to cuddle the creature. Loud noises passed him here and there, but he could not get out. After a while, the leaf loomed, and cricket felt it was time to move to the surface and to look for some more food. Soon the sensation of danger disappeared and blissful ignorance took over. He needed a mate to share his victory; that's the way a cricket demonstrates heroic nature. At the instant when cricket expressed his mating call, a giant shadow loomed above him. The huge creature encircled the cricket in his moment of lax attention.

This time it wasn't the bird returning for her prey; rather it was a boy, searching for a gift. The stranded cricket kicked his legs in alternating thrusts, swinging as if on peddles of a bicycle at fifty miles-per-hour. The cricket heard sudden, loud noises from the mysterious giant that had captured him, yet more loud clamors appeared. The insect did not like the loud noises. His capture meant no mate and no food tonight, but his struggles of escape went on. Bell cricket had not recognized this predator and was confused by his surroundings. There was a sudden darkness during the transfer to some soft surface that didn't feel like the inside of a beak, but rather the inside of a gentler mouth of another predator, maybe. That is what it felt like to be eaten, a sort of conscious thought. It didn't feel bad except hunger was pressing at his being. A sudden light beamed across: the color of grass, a familiar surrounding. The cricket was once again adjusting to a new environment, somewhat larger than the other two. Was he free? Sacrificing his own soulmate, the cricket brought two other souls closer together as a little girl, too, now marveled over the creature. The boy's gift to his crush seemed to finally capture her attention.

Mysterious stranger

Shwoofl-tvob, Shwoofl-tvob, the feet-drags behind me interrupted my thoughts. Oh, I was thinking about how my mother used to tell me, or read to me in a story, about not being too judgmental. Actually I am not, but sometimes our feelings get in the way of our minds. I don't judge my friends by appearance; rather, I judged them for their thoughts, actions, and later our meshing views. Why does the mind work this way? It gives you first impressions and doesn't let you get to know the real person until much later. Others seem to do that to me often. People might think that I am quiet and shy to talk to, and I *am* reserved but don't fall to a particular category as I tend to mesh with an array of personalities. But reality can sometimes go unexpected, then *really* weird things happen.

Shwoofl-tvob, that noise was getting louder. I turned the corner of a deserted short-cut. *Shwoofl-tvob*! I turned around and was startled by a man in a long, black coat. Atop his head was a round, dented hat with a wide brim that covered most of his face. The small amount of skin that peeked out was pale, almost translucent like ice over winter snow, with even paler blotches sprinkled about his corium.[3] His features were emaciated, making him look like a living skeleton

[3] skin.

wrapped in that long coat. Envision a scythe in his hand; why, he would be the image of death!

I suddenly felt little ants run beneath my skin and through most of my body. *Cutis anserina,* my mind recalled with difficulty the medical term for the cold bumps upon my skin. Who was this man? There was no way I had ever seen him before.

Why did he seem to come after me? I turned another corner and quickened my pace from adrenaline powering my legs. With each of his strident steps behind me, I worked harder to increase the parting between us. There, the length of his bony legs was to his advantage. And I was just a child. This must be a coincidence!? He must not want me! I trotted. I heard a yell from behind, "Hey!" See, it was all my imagination. Ha! Yet the call urged me to trot faster. Soon I could feel my lungs expending and cooling from the exertion. Fighting for survival, I was choking like someone on smoke of a forest bonfire. I didn't scream though and waste air as I knew that no one would hear me. I sensed I was alone with this specter of a stranger. And he was chasing after me. Maybe.

I glanced backward and noticed a smirk on his face and how the white of his teeth matched his bleached complexion. His arms were flailing. In rage? I couldn't tell. He stretched like some mummy, catching up and looking like a birch twig in night's darkness rather than welcoming daylight.

I didn't notice his eyes from the shadow of his hat, but I had almost made out two glowing coals. I felt my feet greeting something hard on the cement—not soft earth. The image of the walkway was close when I realized I was about to strike solid ground. When I opened my eyes, at first not knowing where I was, I gained consciousness and realized I was not tied up or taken away. I was simply on the ground, unharmed. Still, when the stranger reached out his hand to grab me, I let out a yelp! When my wits were more about me, I could see that he was helping me up, "You dropped this." I took the wallet he handed to me, which had my school ID in the clear pocket view. I nodded in disbelief, trying to find words as I sought to draw air into my lungs.

"I'm going to be teaching at your school. I just moved here. I think I have you in my English class."

"Thank you," burst out of my mouth, "You scared me with your black coat and that hat! It's hot out!" As he turned to me, I saw his eyes were like beads, not blue or brown, but pink!

"I'm an albino. I have to be very careful in the sun."

I felt embarrassed and very guilty that he ran after me for so long to be only kind and friendly. Well, I could not even look into those pink eyes again, no matter how beautiful they became at that moment. I mean, I ran from him! I mistook him for an awful character while he had the most honorable personality so determined to do the right thing. Maybe I mocked him or assured his doubt towards himself... Yet, partly why I couldn't face him from that point on is because I'm able to enjoy something he cannot: the golden rays of sunlight painting my skin.

Rainbow World

Laughing with the rainbows,
Flying really high,
See the world around us,
Through the big, blue sky.
What it really looks like,
Here from different side,
Other side of rainbows,
Let's go see, let's slide!

Friend 'till End

Friends are meant to be forever,
Reaching the same steps together,
In love and peace,
Even help in trouble,
Never let go hands,
Does this call the meaning of friendship?
So more than that: from depth to tip.

The Magical Night
(version 1)

The crystal, clear night,
The stars—so bright,
The beautiful, shiny snow,
Anywhere you may go.
The charming night,
Oh what a beautiful sight!
The golden moonlight glow,
Upon the shinning snow.
I heard the bells,
On that magical night,
Oh, how sweet the sound,
So gracefully right.

*** ◊ ***

The stars are beautiful tonight.
The glooming sense,
but wondrous sight.
The aroma of a floral ocean,
will circle around your head.
On a night like this,
you can't be sad.

⁂ ◊ ⁂

Magic Night
(version 2)

This crystal and crisp night,
the stars are glowing so bright!
With brilliant and crunchy snow,
wherever you may wish to go.

The Moon is lighting the way.
It's bright outside they say.

The Christmas Eve and all who live
inside Marfin's hut are alive:
The dolls, the berries, and the dust-fly
fairies will awake with envisioning sigh.

This is a magical night,
birthing truly magic delight.

Dreamer

I sleep and I dream of swans on the lake.
I see a beautiful one, a Queen, white, with a crown.
The sun is warm; the air is sweet
with flowers that I take.
Music with flutes all about me make
sounds onto a fabric-less gown.

Oh how good! I needed this break.
I sleep this night in a panoramic mime.
My world of dreams born.
Morning comes, and I awake.
My sleep says, "Good-bye." Was it all fake?
My dreams are gone but 'til next time.

Ocean symphony

I walked to the ocean last night.
The air was thick and liquid,
like a dark, damp tulle.
Moon's yellow, lizard eye
floated over the water.
The sand was powdered sugar
under my feet.
The sound of the waves
was like a giant symphony of
flutes, horns, and strings,
all tuning in at once.

Sunrise

The sun is rising over the ground,
It's the morning time,
I could hear a happy sound,
From the birds,
The sky is fading, unbound.

I filled my lungs with
freshness of atmosphere.
As I ran onto the street,
a little gust passed here.
And, I could feel it at my feet.

⁂ ◊ ⁂

Air: limitless, clingy, and fair,
Sent flurry through my hair,
Seeped warm sense to inside.
Oh what a pleasant ride!

⁂ ◊ ⁂

A Call to Tree

The tree, the tree,
You must be always free.
The tree in the night,
You must be nice.
Wind blows in the night,
I know it's like pressure and ice.
But girl near you sits,
No loneliness fits.
The tree, the tree,
You can be almost free!

*** ◊ ***

A Girl Summer

Summer is coming
on a beautiful carriage.
In her hair—a green ribbon,
in her hand, she has a flower,
and a rose that blooms
when she carries her power.

Summer has on a dress,
which blows in the wind
and touches the ground,
This dress turns to grass.
She speaks to animals around.

Animals love the girl Summer,
They stay next to her, humming,
and when she's coming…every
itsy-bitsy plant blooms at her coming.

And, all little children love Summer.
They wait to play and relax with her.
"Summer 's coming!" is the usual murmur.

Autumn

Autumn, autumn, autumn,
Why are you so sad?
The leaves are falling,
But I want to be glad.

Autumn, autumn, autumn,
Summer 's gone away.
Surely, you are here to stay.

Autumn, autumn, autumn,
The quiet wind is blowing,
And left the leaves a'falling.

And autumn! Autumn, stay with me.
We will wait the winter together.
And, once you hear me calling,
We'll get over that harsh weather.

No more worries troubling your head.
Just dancing angels guarding there instead.
A silent wish so perfect that does not require a word.
I love you, Parents, by our actions that shall well be heard.
Truth, love, and kindness shall mix.
For that is God's most cherished fix.
Let fortune in your heart and purse,
Express pure joy, which one cannot rehearse.
I hope that you accept these beats of grateful heart.
So, thank you very much for your loving, parenting art.

⁂ ◊ ⁂

Birthday Wish

I'll make a card, up from my heart.
A wish come true, good birthday too.
I'll reach to the sky,
and grab a rainbow or two.
So, Happy Birthday to you!

This is the card, out of my heart,
a wish in a box,
and a dream in your socks.
This day should be special to you,
and to friends, great and few.

How Sky loved the Sun

The golden Sun came to the Sky.
It smiled but sent warmth in rife.
Sky brightened, away with the wry.
A visit from edgeless ocean of life
insisted love will forever remain.

The Sun is still there,
arm-rays touching us.
Sky's heart is though bare
because of Sun's pass.

"The Sun will still love you,"
said loud voice of fairy,
ringing through the clouds
to sparrows words carry.

A sunset is coming;
The Sky is now dark.
The Sun's warm feeling
is still in our hearts.

An Angel of love came to the Sky.
There's joy in the world;
The Sun has come up.
Hugging, kissing, they twirled.
The day's cry turned to chirrup.

Old-time Mythology

Once upon a time
in the beginning,
where God created all,
would you believe that all was ordered
—straight as two dots running a line.
Everyone naturally got along.
Knew when to come; no need to call.
The life was long,
and people chose to leave the world,
and go to a better place
to closer be with the Lord.

There was no sickness.
There was peace and love
and mostly no stillness.
There's a party or a show.
If lovers wanted a family, they'd
plant a seed and care for the root
and watch the tree grow.
But anyone could.
And, soon it stretched its arms
(not weapons but branches),
sensed the cool draft
and the birds' singing.

Anyone missing a love's departing
shall count from one to ten.
Similar human drawing first oxygen
thus has a great life starting.

⁂ ◊ ⁂

Rose Blooms

A flower opened with the sun,
On the sunrise morning.
Smile, Flower, for it's fun.
Blooms she petals showing.

Everybody says, "Look it's a rose!
May I have her? May?
Surely, I'll propose."

Start dark night.
And rose close,
Sleep her petals,
Sleep her clothes.

Everybody says, "Look it's a rose!
May I take her? May?
I would not impose."

Stand up, Rose, it's early morning.
She proudly showed her eyes.
Silly, how her skirt is turning.
She, certainly, grew in size.

Everybody says, "Wish I had this rose!"
"Pay to take her? Pay?
Why would you suppose!"

*** ◊ ***

The Rose

Rose near garden
each time расцвела.[4] Flower, it's for
Dear Bella,
Father says to Mom.
Lower cried girl in her room
on the bed.
Why is the birthday bad?
Earlier she said all's fine.
Ordinary, nothing out of line.
Twinkle in Bella's eye read,
"What a special gift of mine!"

---

[4] расцвела: rastsvela (Ru)--blossomed

⁂ ◊ ⁂

Heart Sweet

Quiet…just listen to the sounds of your heart:
the way it plays a perfect beat.
That dancing melody just sings,
the way acceptance goes from warmth
to heat.

The choice is yours; the heart is young.
Those flutes and drums just never stop.
A new chill covers you inside,
the heart keeps going…hop
and hop.

Place of Imagination

(a lullaby to my sister)

There once was a beautiful place

that had sparkling diamonds falling from space.

There once was a place where grains of sand tickled feet

and waters that hugged children, who didn't go in too deep.

There once was a beautiful place that had flowers.

They fell everywhere in tendering showers.

I'm not sure but I was once told

that this special place was covered in gold.

That place is right here next to your dreams

and could be reached by a talent it seems.

That talent is your imagination,

which turns all dreams into sensation!

Teenage

What burning day has brought to geond sills?
With firing passion fought the big, red giant,
Crept up to warn over bright hills,
And fired at the combat like a soldier fire-ant...

⁂ ◊ ⁂

Await, wrapped in some wool,
for feast.

A visit from the autumn's breeze
swirled up some magic for the season's stew,
threw in some pumpkins there too,
and then to cease the heat, he mighty-power blew

to east
and meant to let it cool...

On-S-T

There's no truth on Earth,
and that's the truth, you see.
Real matter buried underneath,
beside the big, dark tree
of one's mind.
Let me save you the time
in realizing this true find...

*** ◇ ***

Shame Game

Shame to those,
whose jealous ways cause weapons to sprout.
Shame to those,
whose jealousy itself brought up to creep in-out.
But, those who hold no shame at all
are ones to think about.

Red Moon

The gestures of the moon have faded

washed out through the busy urban street,

which shut the moon's warm features meant to greet.

Time morphing dark embroidery on skyline dinner banquet,

the one enchanting guests, indeed,

and used to make them want to eat,

to washed-out veil locking in disgrace glum host's face

...

by the same city rays which laid it.

No longer was the moon allowed to speak

true wondrous secrets that it used to hold--

trusting a young soul trapped within a corpse that's old

--whose sailors gloried under infinite, black blanket

reduced to present treatment from a heart turned cold.

They garbled precious secrets; distance bridged the bold.

Staccato sign left mindless passer not a trace of moon's face

...

while claret stained a moon, as would a wine leak.

*** ◊ ***

White Muliebrity

And dare *I* say that the winter's brutal
with all the majesties that glisten in that sea
and have the capabilities to mute all.
For what the purpose claims to fall from thee?

When there appeared young pigsney storming,
hath dropped or sprinkled something by the frozen bay.
Shall I compare her to a winter's morning?
Or do I need to say a summer's day?

The white bellibone hath just entered
a garden lovely, truth, as she.
Untouched by human presence, she came and centered,
displayed shy innocence, (impurity) free.

[Herman Melville]

How chansonly came the next Ulman sound!
The snow kept pulsing with poetic rhythms.
In time, sun kissed thy holy ground
that made flakes dazzle-dance like prisms.

*T*oday she roams that sacred garden.
*R*ough times have passed that made it such,
*U*ntil we see and seek for pardon…
*E*ey! For which upon that poetry can say so much…

In Great Hands

The magic rises through the foggy day,
throughout the dawn that brings a new bright ray,
while reddish sky turns orange-pink
and passes hope, which only light can bring.

On this fine wonder sun just smiles and kisses day
and people's joy comes out to play. Horay!
And, gentle breeze then blows a kiss.
God's wonder it can give with bliss.

You're in great hands, which stretch to evermore
because a molecule of Him is the whole universe's core.

Another Battle

Half a story we heard
clearly missing a word.
Thinking right as we are.
Didn't get very far.

We went battling our foes
hearing only our woes.
Should we heard their cry,
we would give them a try.

Many days have gone by
having lived midst a lie.
We just walk on our toes.
Try not fall or it shows.

Simply stand like a czar!
Clamed he never touched tar.
We behaved like a bird
when we're part of a herd.

The Greatest Enemy as Gift

Wise-men riddle to make wise with words,

for they are sure to escape free as birds.

But, a word cannot compare to a bird at all!

A bird could come back, you see,

but a word has escaped and be it[5]...

Oh! What does a word represent?

But a single word is interlocked between the

Palmae leaves of peasant.

A word shuns upon itself like a single note in overture.

It stains like an oil stroke over canvas,

vanishes as magician's strong impressions.

Those crafts cannot be in a midst repeated.

The mouth of letter 's waxed to be defeated.

A word is like a claw toying a prey.

It is a hungry beast enjoying a mistaken seal feast.

It permanently prints a scorching scarlet fire unto flesh.

---

5 Though a strong urge to say "let be" here, this line wasn't meant to rhyme.

Those are the words that leave a scar

with kind of gabble taken way too far.

⁂ ◊ ⁂

Fly on the Window

Something, like a tiny fly, clasped onto netted window.
Grids passing through the amber corpus
reveal symmetry in the design.
Perked at one point is something like a crown
diverging into two from one,
as if a crafty mouth divided over impious decision--or hissing.
Yellow tones picked for the background, full of hazy medley.
Upon its small rest, it defies nature's intensions.
The coronal trace upright flows king's cape to the side.
Bottom border curved up giving depth to the sight.
Soft currents of the outside force it to stir.
And then, it's strong again upright, holding tight,
presenting its power in all its minuscule.
Body fades again to dark and frozen
and barefaced upon my viewing portal.
I get closer… and it flies.

⁂ ◊ ⁂

A Flaky Story

The white, furry coat spread across the ground.
This beautiful snow
turned to sparkling glow.
Everything was motionless, quiet, no sound.

Flakes embedded starlight as tiny gems onto whiteness.
This moment became indulging.
Through the coating, the truth is bulging…
Each point of snow is immersed with lightness.

Each trail uncovers a page of a story…
The steps I take are showing.
Truth over snow is growing.
And I see other prints, alone, make history.

Just Sleep

Fall to the trap of unconscious possession,
the parallel world of frozen intention,
where dominant power shuts down any thought.
Save willful possessions, which sunshine has brought!
Yet, calmness of balance slows down regression.
Then, mind entraps where the battle was fought.

Let circuit rewire each milestone track,
where alternate routs are destined to hack.
Soft ripples of wakefulness circle away.
A record starts rolling for quests of the day.
Small portal of warm holes shine beyond fine jack.
A chance to pick paths is your last thought to say.

Poly-eyed

Eyes unfilled with turquoise fluid
stared back through the feathery solid.
Cries came of creature in sparing rhythms.
Cared she for the behemoth in front.

Volts of compassionate fear fired her face.
His eyes, cinctured in gold, brightened.
Bolts apart she's from the wondrous vision.
Is she motionless? Hypnotized by his presence?

Others passing did not witness such beauty.
Opening his cape, he unveils to her his pulchritude.
Mothers around grabbing hold of their children.
Listening to his internal opaqueness, only she's hearing.

Somewhere between the many eyes,
two less impressive expressed solemn surprise.
There the peacock told her his tale,
to answer questions of mistook male beauty.

Something of Nothing

The long awaited moment is here...
Each petal's slight movement observed.
Red velvet and silk almost moving in fear.
Yet, truly that thought is obscured.

Stern coating is gently moving apart
with elegant grace peaking through.
This marvelous sight represents work of art
while dew crystals proving this true.

In moment the flower is garbed in fine jewels
that sprinkle the rays of all color in glory.
Simple winsomeness notably covered in wealth.
Yet, remains allure beneath each accessory.

Sabrina

I told you that you were a jewel, Sabrina.
I'm right, my sparkling ballerina.
Not only your smile will light up the room,
but also your mind will brighten your groom.

Your kindness, too, forever will shine.
Your charm and your talents are really divine.
Not to mention your looks always sharp as the cut.
You're as gorgeous inside as the brilliant's gut.

There is but a thing that truly won't match.
Your warmness is felt which the crystal can't catch.
But like the jewel you'll always be crystal clear
through hidden complexity one needs to fear.

A Timely Thought

Let time freeze!
What is time?
After all it can tell…

The clock-maker fell.
Fell for Mystery.
Is it her that's abstract?

Space dares to distract.
Unpredictable squeeze…
Can one really define?

All is fine!
No time to yell.
Wait another century.

⁂ ◊ ⁂

Wind

The wind chimed away past the trees of a willow.
He stormed into cracks and over wide hills.
With soft embrace as if fleece on a pillow,
he rolls along with dust creating broadside mills.

His mighty, broad squeeze can harm trembling giants.
Traversing each day, he aims for piece of mind.
In gloom or scattered smiles alike brilliants,
he comes about fast then ceases behind.

He comes during cries of saddening clouds.
Then brings about his presence within play dates around.
With each heart-felt blow to the maddening sprouts,
he searches about until gates are found.

Some days he will tease many younglings,
as if engaging with fanciful play.
Reaching wide he strolls alleys, walks amblings.
He rescues a hot morning to give a pleasant day.

He whispers, he howls, he roars.
Wind gently shifts about and spies.
Loud singing wakes owls and boars
soon reveals his presence without surprise.

Star Pirate

Just look upward and maybe you will see him.
Star Pirate standing tall and trim,
a face that Blackbeard wouldn't think to come near.
In his time he infected quite a few with fear.
As student that Sir Isaac loved to teach,
he once dreamed soon to stars he'd reach.
It seemed to happen overnight,
he went away on a mysterious flight.
Mysteriously, also, he appeared,
but to a foreign place he cleared.
He didn't know then where he belonged.
But, heart showed him for what he longed.

Life

Atoms,
Create molecules.
Each perfectly pasted.
Sequence of synchronous work.
Together they ascend toward power.
Choreographed stage position follows specific roles.
Communication bridges any unknown, complex, false situations.
Mistakes are reduced toward minimum, yet clearly made.
Devastations materialize in community when one thing goes wrong.
How does life continue when something does go wrong—it is a superior marvel?!

Morning Run

Morning run

Upon my travelled ways I find myself
the trace of my run ends carefully
unraveling over far body toward connecting not known
of sand beyond still expanse to everything
hour sweeps sour weeps wherein earth awaking.

⁂ ◊ ⁂

Ballet

I feel my internal machinery charge.
Large open space is mine to take.
Flake would describe me better now.
How light and spontaneous I flow indeed!
Feed to the music the graceful component.
Sonnet of visual senses is stirring.
Luring the audience, I have something to tell.
Fell into trance to the core of my mood.
Stood from their seats with focus sharp as spear.
Hear no one, I morph into feeling expressed.
Impressed with my journey, they see me fly across.
Cross that fine line of a realistic dream.
Cream movements taken to thank the Lord.
Sword gestures cutting the air in return.
Churn coils forming to stage softly preaching.
Reaching as far as the body could.
Would world once again appreciate art?
Heart pours away 'til the calmness of end.
Friend, thank you for sharing this joy!

Phone Call

A woman, past forty, still rests by the phone,
where years of grim streaks have left her alone.
Impatience and dullness oft crosses her eyes,
which implants a layer to her frequent lies.
Her deepest concern is the nails on her hands.
She whirls them tightly times when she pretends.
Forced smile is added to paint on her face.
It's rare she'll jiggle her weight off her place.
Her body now shriveled like plum in the sun.
She's told to act nicely as if she has fun.
A noise still stirs her as she preps what to say.
Claw grabbing the phone, "May I help you today?"

A man trips while walking to somewhere away.
He mildly falls into puddle of clay.
He's hurt and defeated by game of his fate.
Please help citizen or he might be late.
Passing pedestrians came not chivalrous.
They plastered looks sharper than his nasty boss.
A car soon came round the corner too fast.
Man's mind flashed forward to time in his cast.
He closed his eyes for a moment to pray.
Not too soon in a minute the car turned away.
He thought should he call and reached where phone lay.
And answered wrong call, "May I help you today?"

*** ◊ ***

Sport

Hurry, it's approaching!
Wind gust before the flying ball.
Acing the tough shot due to great coaching.
A high jump stops ball from crossing the wall.

Awesome, the powerful shot!
Requires patient ....concentration.
Peace after realization of player training a lot.
Strained facial muscle reads mental preparation.

Hit, ball makes a thump!
The racket recoils.
Quick here, take that next jump!
That other flying clump was the soil's.

Whoosh, coolness...
The wind cheers the other team.
It ceases a moment of foolishness.
Or, so to make it seam.

Hahh, fight for joy!
A great player excels under pressure.
This is the game not a child's toy.
To keep both at hand for right moment is treasure.

Shwoo, call for help…
A part of success is the given ability.
Each improved triumph is met with a yelp.
Just what an impressive agility.

Yay, the ball is not the enemy here.
Rather greeted each time with guidance.
It's time we let the other side fear.
All body motions express years of experience.

Wow, the movement becomes like a dance!
Power-packed yet graceful and planned.
Natural and strategic placement of stance.
And most of all, fears are canned.

Across that climb is mirrored dedication.
An inspiration come alive.
The victorious hand-eye coordination.
A sport teaching the skill of life…

⁂ ◊ ⁂

The Healing Power of Rain

In light of morning,
the gentle summer's rain
has drizzled last of its long strain.
If it has never rained upon these grounds,
then they would be called deserts.
The ones that easily could drown,
in spite of wearing a bright crown.
The heart of it just lightly pounds:
untamed, unlearned, unblessed by God's arms,
dry.

Then there would be more sense to cry.
Instead, let's turn toward sun, let's grow, let's fly!
Just try.

The more it covers ground early with glisten,
the less a chance it would fulfill its duty later
and drop by.

It may change course and listen
to your simple warning.

M*ind* **O***n* **M***odel*

Courage swept through as
a quiet Zephyr
Braveness gleaming in her face
hard to decipher
I have not witnessed one to match
her wit
I have not seen matched intuition like
her mind lit
Her love cannot be expressed
in words
The talents flowing out
in herds
Gentle epitome of beauty paints
her trim stature
I thank you Lord if part of her genetic code
my DNA can capture!

Reflected Beauty

Beauty-true overwater ensued
Reflection as fine as nature around
Running toward water long tresses behind
In spite opposing forces, great purpose pursued
Rising above boulders becoming unbound
Yet featured expression is ever so kind
Lone ripples seen from smile after a pleasant whiff
Surrounding aqua blurs the moment's picture
Then once again all clear to the gemstone mind
Slender frame supports every valley and cliff
Feeling wonderful before such a fixture
Showing stance of something so royal
Lips as pink as a communicating sky
Hurry to feast eyes on her amidst a green mixture
Glowing features highlight temper as loyal
Not too many like that make one cry
Skin too supple and smooth texture jellyfish-like
Not flourished by camouflage but revealed in glory
Like waterfall nonetheless generates energy spike
Drips echo of nature so beautiful, never pry.

Reflected Beauty cont.

Ensued over water true beauty
Around nature as fine as reflection
Behind long tresses and toward running water
Despite opposition, pursued purpose forces duty
Bound but rising above in protection
Kind of expression featuring else broader
A whiff reduces pleasant scene to a lonely ripple
Picturesque surroundings momentarily turn blurry
Mind not the gem (wind), for absence clearly feels hotter
Valued cliffs support as the frame becomes dripple
Fixed before wonderful feeling of flurry
Royal something, though hidden, stance showing
Sky communicating to a flower's pink lip
Mixture of greenery prepares for feast in a hurry
Loyal features of light temporally high glowing
Not that sorrowful cry makes one but many of likes let it slip
Like jellyfish texture smooth yet supple to skin
Glory revealed but camouflage flourished
Spikes of energy generated from the waterfall within
Never pry the beautiful nature of which echoes drip...

⁂ ◊ ⁂

To My Mentors...

You built a strong highway
on which I could travel.
Now a journey awaits me toward Mr. Gray.
Thank you for laying that initial gravel,
letting me choose the wisest way!

You bestowed me with a meticulous map
and sent me with sagacious instructions along.
I'm finally adorned in my gown and cap.
Though journey was grueling and long,
you've made it worthy by bridging the gap!

Mamochka

I'll grace your mind with inspiration
about a very precious girl.
I gained a feeling of admiration
strictly by chance of observation
not in a bias whirl.

You may have guessed already,
but here's another clue:
I truly love her dearly—
a love designed steady—
never to go off, it is true.
Let me describe more clearly...

My mother is my first great teacher.
She is my last accounted advice.
Each page to her is treated as a feature.
She praises me at any moment; Lets me rise.

Sects

Creeping...toward the jagged corner,
serpent hall, unwinds tangled mess
as rags infuse room in frore, murky cave milieu
like some stalactite about to engulf fleshy stew.
Much of room is clocked, teasing pawns of a one-sided chess,
thriving in itself as rat's free garner.

There, under massive spider lead chains,
immured gateway mutters seldom shrill.
Brave will enter; those appalled will flee.
Inquiry sets, but—tension aside—so do we.
The ambience spills a container of chill,
at the sight of *them* our life fluid drains.

And we hear again once we gain our hue:
It is laughter, intrigue, and lightheartedness,
strewing out of a face more charred than a burner.
Gathered munchkins about the mystic sojourner
florid stories flowed from each, to the best of my guess,
of their journeys to other worlds no one knew.

Only, one was still silent, pushed away carelessly.
It's this kind of behavior that no doubt makes one ill.
Finally, up from the corner, with the strength that remains
—on a good day she's lucky to have a few grains—
softly, she spoke of her own embarked foreign thrill
about Land of the butterfly, dragonfly, and a bug lady.

At the end of her tale, their reactions turned meaner.
Why, to see simple insects, prompts no foreign ingress!
Wasting moments of view about something that flew...
Same, no time or breath worth convincing their brains
that half dragon-half fly and a buttery wing showed more
etiquette skill.
Well, it isn't too late to get back, the wise Lady-bug would
agree.

Integrity (inter-greedy)

Selfless love is really not that selfless
unless you strip away the conscious thought,
but here's something to address:
we often think what one must do as ought.
But, is our duty to ourselves counted as less
important: the answer that humanity has sought.

The problem lies within our mind.
Solution to this no one able yet to find.

Integrity to ourselves always gained
because what makes us is what some strive for.
Since mind from ancient quandary is yet remained,
key to conundrum we have bore.
But maybe somewhere, someone has obtained
a piece that's deeply hidden to the core.

We draw caricature from our existence,
then, look away into the distance.

I. Colour series

Firry passion evinced from cavernous florid.
Fooling cupid to force love to admire thee.
Teaser ties over the secrets it may flash in.
Incredible style gathers thoughts to believe inst.
Indicative spread of burning aggression but air of Rome.
Readily proposes its pallet to have earnest.
Except, forgets strokes and opposes path to ignore it.

red

II. Colour series

Richness of hue replaces longed peace.
Respect wraps the thinker aside its fine threads.
Calmness is birthing each speck to each crease.
Brave, tangible entrancement strolls aboard dreads.
All points and all lines flow into each other
then spread every light as if floating above ground.
Same particle-waves merge and tease one another
that stole red-and-yellows to purposely astound.

III. Colour series

So sweetly awaking its youthful strokes,

bright branches of sunshine escaped soak to glow.

Came deeper enchantment than morning of light.

Every ray, dot of subject jumps as a leaper.

Turns these scolding teeth into joy sculpted ivory.

Leaves beams mind-engulfed after one sees and learns.

Gay excitement collaborates what nerve receives.

So fantastic to be part of this color play!

yellow

Stairwell

Tame excitement!
creases to blame.
again ceases
What we sought to regain

scope we hope to retain.
obtain upper slope:
enticing domain,
Enlightenment arising,

Victim

The bitterly sharp flavor of woe finalized its atmospheric diffusion. Upon instinct, the epithelial cells of Clyde's body experienced unexplainable, intrusive tension. Yet, the crisp, readable air—in the essence that one can sense the grooves and moisture of gas clusters like braille readers sense grooves—was not the root of Clyde's discomfort. Another scent, which pierced more than the sharp stones under his bare feet, lingered in the air. The aroma was faintly fresh from someone's cologne yet covered a stale, careless facade of flesh. Another pass of the wind confirmed the fragrance when the air thrust molecules over Clyde's beaten and deformed face. Dewy awareness of someone's presence loomed inside Clyde's cognition. Clyde Golggi ordinarily would confront a predicament and battle to either side's final heart pump, but recently, the "new Clyde" approached to solutions with the guidance of his legs more eagerly than with the murmurs of his heart. He turned away from the cologne scent and urged for the moment epinephrine fills his feeble bloodstream. Prevailing over his hopes, a sundered thought appeared around Clyde's aura: Maybe I should submit to fate and forget the trace of hope that I still house? Still, he longed for placidity and spurned the idea of interaction with any stranger, so he began running into nowhere.

He had a sense of familiarity in this place. Everything smelled and sounded native, but these senses were barren and stygian.

The bumpy ground massaged blisters into the soles of his feet. Tapered whiff melded into the surrounding aura. The nature's elaborate perfume, filled with natural and artificial vim, is more comparable to orchestra's bass notes and overtones rather than to a novel color blend of an abstract painting. The run amassed pain to several senses: Emotional pain became the base for physical pain on feet, lungs, heart, nose; this added to the drought and irritation in his mouth. Each breath declined in quality and quantity while the ground seemed to incline as the sprint progressed. A feeling of uncontrollable feet was meant to frighten Clyde Golggi and done so with enough persuasion to entrap Clyde—by own mind. The will to run persisted, but the feet lagged in efficiency. This raised frustration to more passion than a downhill chase after a rolling cart. The awareness of his potential wouldn't forgive the power machine's lack of execution; performing under worst self-standards is a formidable spirit-absorber and drains the confidence of even the strong. This significant ambush was enough to curb Clyde. But, after all, his core didn't halt him—as didn't the many previous attempts of this small, stubborn part of mind.

"Wait!" A deep voice reached from behind. Its echo was quite deafening. He's been waiting long enough. The voice sounded familiar, yet Clyde couldn't identify it. The environment felt to be deflating over the helpless lamb centered in chaos. He heard more calls, but perception of the surroundings faded momentarily. A deep, internal connection advised him to stop and face the direction from where he started. Every sensation resurfaced into Clyde Golggi.

Vision was the finale to cascaded progress toward regaining functional sensation. At last, he *saw* the surroundings. Nothing beautiful for a general observer, but a rush of good energy dispersed through Clyde's body. The pleasant feeling fled when he spotted a distant, distinct figure. He winced at knowing the origin of that distorted voice. Crowning its silhouette were shades of grey sky and beige ground sprinkled with abandoned, tawny twigs and rocks. Passed that, his gaze focused back on the central point, from where emerged his old colleague, whom Clyde once tagged as friendly.

Finally, Clyde had a definitive reason behind what his instinct started. Clyde's determination ruled him to flee with strength not explored in the previous sprint. With this mindset, Clyde's passion materialized into action. However, upon a turn, any chances of escape dissolved with the startling discovery of a blocked road, and he was tugged by opposing forces. Clyde's heart felt accelerated; still, his feet skidded across grains of sand. The ground turned to be not a flat piece of desert but a rocky mountain, and he neared an edge: the edge of the world, apparently. Why fate has come to determine this as his ending way? A rush of air rose along his length....

***

One of Clyde's long legs slammed atop a wooden footboard of his bed, and his initially hazy awareness was instantly altered to full comprehension due to a shock escalation across that leg. He realized that nothing has changed. The contortion in his face derived from pain, yet no manifestation of it bothered him as did the disappointing feeling somewhere in the bulk of his amygdala[6]. Emptiness and regret persisted until he found enough strength to extinguish the feeling. Last night was the first time in almost five years that his dreams animated. Vivid visions developed toward the end of his dream, but he vehemently craved never to leave that state of 'virtuality,' despite it being considered a nightmare. That dream snickered at what became his life. His desires were tethered slightly past his reach...Aside from the disappointment, he felt frustration and some form of inconclusiveness. He shifted away from the footboard and lay on the pillow with intention of resuming the visions—but was unable to induce sleep. The time was open for contemplation, which one should know that often thoughts carry a dream astray from its embarking. Thus, he created the contrary to the preferred effect. He formed a habit to empty thinking these days because discouragement and confusion seemed to fill most of his waking time, and no one around knew how to listen. Everyone 'listened'; but no one *cared* to listen. Even pure empathy unsolidifies through freedom of escape. He did have but one person to really hear him, though: himself... ■

---

[6] An emotional center in the brain (temporal lobe) that is suggested to be involved in olfactory pathways.

***

Without proper retro-vision, one can't achieve good listening. Clyde's current outlook relies on a key event in his background. Before the cornerstone, Clyde was not simply Clyde Golggi. For seven years of his life, he carried a title of something other than plain Clyde. During last five years after that, Clyde hasn't dared to utter those proper nouns as he thought that he lost ownership to his name and anything associated with it. A defining part of himself was missing and reminded him everyday that it was. Yet, his supporters cared for him—as long as they didn't have to spend long hours surrounded by his solemn reality. I guess, finally, Clyde felt to be a victim of the direction his life turned ...It wasn't a wonder that *she* wasn't as close to him anymore, especially since Clyde acted defeated. After losing his sight five years earlier, he was unable to perform tasks that defined his caring, witty, independent character-type. Over seven years deserving an honored title and the strength he thought he had was false power—and understanding that was the only positive of the accident. Then he lost touch with the world and himself. So this is to say that Clyde's usual personality was affected. No, this new weakness was not his nature at all.

Under previous conditions, Dr. Golggi wouldn't let a negative thought pass, but he hadn't seen a bright future for over three months. Nothing was bright or dim, anyway, since he was blinded—in both sight and reality, yet his happy personality didn't cease so abruptly but rather abated with time. And this may be a flaw...but he didn't try covering his distress with elaborate acting, rather he wore emotions over his body and on his face, yet that was just the surface. The bottom of the island of hopelessness was sealed internally. This, of course, took a toll on his relationships.

But the sink hole for Dr. Golggi, as any man would coin, commenced upon his courageous stroll through city's air. The wind was not kind to flesh that day; the thrusting clumps of molecules fiercely massaged passers' confronting halves and teased with loose clothing. Thus, after *feeling* the weather, Dr. Golggi attired the infamously ubiquitous grey coat. The harsh wind seized opportunity to further carve the tender areas near Clyde's facial scars and tug at the thick, black hair, now meeting the shoreline of skin farther up his crown than originally destined. This collective expression—the creased scars and damaged hairline—aged him almost twofold. Besides his resistance to relying on a crutch, he was forced to take his cane. Needless to say, Clyde—with his props—illuminated as the point of attention, even in the urban setting. However, the fast-pace of the city caused the locals to miss a little spec in the spacious city, leaving mostly the children and some tourists to grimace and quiver at the sight of the man. Contradicting with pedestrians' lack of attention, an aerial view of the street presented a stream of droplets separating at a sight of obtrusion and rejoining behind—sort of symbolizing a stream of vital blood droplets bypassing a clot; but perhaps, Dr. Golggi was more like a rock in muddy waters, considering an experience like his would make one stronger. That embodiment of a rigid rock in a downhill stream was once the popular Dr. Golggi, now during the walk, he was observed as a nuisance: funny turn that life has taken. Fair for him that he couldn't see that, but a whistling boy from behind noticed, who grieved for the poor man. Stopping where pavement ends—crossing when the surrounding gusts of body-heat accelerate and narrow plastic sounds resume pulsation on asphalt, Clyde reluctantly admitted relying on his stick for most accurate predictions of couple feet ahead. Those clamors that Clyde produced came with a cost to the public, though; indeed, the nearby saunterers were vexed—grunting. Frustration in the public arose not due to gaudy lady pumps (which for guidance, Clyde acoustically interpreted) but from the source of Clyde's main aid. The next billow of air accompanied a cozy whiff of home cooking, and the smell continued to accumulate. A young male, dorsally[7] to Clyde, softly moaned. Each steam-puff warmed Clyde's face and cycled between pealing away to uncover the frost and pleasantly shocking with incoming tease. Like Clyde, anyone passing undoubtedly had a layer of mist compressing the exposed skin. That was expected; however, metal guardrails midst a sidewalk—Clyde didn't account for, and it happened that his rod missed it, too. He tumbled over the rail and landed—with painful bursts—among debris coating some plastic mat. Clyde felt around for the staff, but no matter where he palpated, everything his fingers tickled over was of homogeneous, filmy synthetic cloaking the cold ground. He didn't hear wood landing because women's startling shills

---

[7] A medical term for 'behind.'

dominated his consciousness. He arose through mumbles piercing the atmosphere, and then a fast beating of feet crescendoed. “Get away from here you low-life slime! This is a Church gathering! Stealing food, huh? Insanity or laziness doesn’t excuse you from sin,” the man made his case public when he jostled Clyde along some direction away from the steam.

A soft force landed on Dr. Golggi’s shoulder, which he mistook for the tarrying throb. “I’m sorry, sir, to see that things like that still happen. May I offer lunch at a café?—It’s a step-up treatment,” a young voice, with the same salty tone as the boy’s from Clyde’s earlier walk, exclaimed.

At first, Clyde hesitated to reply, then Clyde’s visage shifted toward exhibiting content, “Oh no, young man. I’m treating *you* with food and coffee. Lead the way!” After some conversation, Dr. Golggi deduced that this was, indeed, the same gentleman that whistled behind Dr. Golggi, since the boy was able to describe to Clyde of the surroundings and of people’s reactions.

“Luckily, this food is more wholesome than that heart-clogging barbecue they had out,” the youth noted. Dr. Golggi discovered that Mr. Cory was a medical student in town for his studies. Cory wasn’t familiar with this upscale, organic bistro, which had an external wing with French-inspired decor. The white, metal chairs included padding because often the customers used the diner as a meeting spot, and the restaurant provided their own potted greens, spread throughout the patio to create a comfy atmosphere. But, Dr. Clyde Golggi's impression of the bistro's design was limited to the cool curlicues of the surrounding metal. A medley of pleasant smells seeped to the outside, seducing many travelers. Dr. Golggi bought salads and baked fish before they enjoyed a cup of coffee with a couple of pastries.

"Indeed, you'll be a fi-i-ne doctor," Dr. Golggi bobbed his head in pleasure. He outlined the seven years of his surgical practice, but there was no need to mention his job title because as soon as Dr. Golggi introduced himself, the young student's eyes beamed.

"...A poor med student never refuses an opportunity for a free coffee. Thank you; it's a treat." Mr. Cory took a sip of his coffee and cupped his palms around the warm mug, "I can't believe I'm sitting next to you engaged in a conversation! You're like a celebrity—a legend! It depends on our values., but most people fall into distorted admiration of reality stars and entertainment, yet that has no barring on what kind of people we raise to the podium. What are the real traits we value? Meanwhile, the top and dedicated med students learn of leaders, intellects, philanthropists of whom we are certain for what exactly is their fame. Since medicine is actually my passion, I believe this meeting is the highest celebrity opportunity bestowed upon me."

"Well thank you for elevating me to your admiration status. But really, there is a surprising number of great doctors. For the several bad, you'll find an exceptional one."

"There are great doctors, and there are giant pioneers. Once you're world-wide—very few are—you're exceptional!"

Cory noticed a newly formed pink streak over Dr. Golggi's jaws, which clearly didn't present from a chill.

"Thank you, young man. I feel like it's all worth in the end."

Cory grinned, "It's definitely worth it. I mean, you redefined the clinical structure and made things more patient-friendly. I really do admire you for that, even more so than other modern practitioners. You're not just *a* doctor, you're *the* doctor to meet.

"Like the stuff we read about you is incredible! I can't believe that you corrected your mentor's cutting technique. How did that feel?"

"I wasn't correcting him to be rude. I accepted consequence and also made *sure* that he knew it was a suggestion. You know that I was thinking about the patient more than anything else. I was lucky to find the flaw in the much taught technique and correct it...and have my mentor not kill me in the process."

When doctor Golggi speaks, one feels that he is someone of importance, yet no one would find the physical root to that impression as Dr. Golggi is outmost mellow and generous. People might think that he's passive, but in fact, he listens to the words people use. At any point, if there is an oral attack on him, he artfully makes the attacker feel triumph among actual loss.

"The best part is that I see your ingenious idea all the time on my surgery rounds. Many students don't pause to think that it wasn't always like that. Someone had to invent it...

You know, I also notice a lot of tension between staff and doctors. I remember reading that you didn't have any problems and being amazed. You had an unbelievable team relationship. I don't think they had a single bad thing to say. Complete one-eighty degrees from the other docs," Cory slid a hand across the table.

"It's true. The staff team gets overlooked in the midst of one's own greatness. They too had to go to school. Most care as much or more about the patient as the treating physicians. How can we miss the importance of our partners, such as the nurses, when without them, it makes it close to impossible or really difficult to complete the job… Or even, radiologists and anesthesiologists…"

"I know. I hear a lot of stories!"

"Yeah, imagine the practice without them. You probably studied how terrible the conditions were for the patient in the past."

"Oh yes, doctor!"

"A colleague told me about one of his nurses—ooh, he was a brute! —One day she had enough of abuse and brought him a sample of what he asked from her… Except, it wasn't exactly what he requested. He wanted to make sure the nurse fed a baby properly, so she brought him proof, a whole *diaper* full of proof, right to his desk! Nice gift. I wanted to congratulate her. What confidence!" Cory squirmed, and they both laughed.

"Can I ask you something?" Cory's statement momentarily lit sparks in a deep, wide radius around Clyde's heart.

Dr. Golggi lowered his chin and tightened his forehead then almost immediately relaxed, "Sure. Ask away."

"I didn't really want to go into this, but what ...uhm...what's it like being blind?" This is the question Clyde really hoped people would avoid: His character craved constant work and blindness limited him, so he felt resentment and unease toward his 'condition.' Clyde's major facial muscles contracted further than that of a lemon-licking child. The tension traveled down the body, and Clyde felt his arm muscles protrude. Clyde was lucky to have his coat on because Cory would have noticed the well-sculpted arm muscles defining the areas of stress.

"Maybe I shouldn't have asked you that," Cory stumbled in regret.

"No, I should talk." Dr. Golggi took a moment to relax. "Look, can you wiggle your ears?"

"No."

"Neither can I, but I bet that gentleman sitting to the side of us can. Maybe he is one of fifteen percent of population to inherit this formerly useful trait."

"How did you know it was a man? He hasn't spoken once since we sat here!"

"Lucky guess. That, and women tend to sit with their legs close together due to conditioned response to dress code. When I heard the metallic table legs ring quite sequentially, I got my first clue. It's lunch-time, so it's likely that a business person is taking a lunch break. Thus on a chilly day, it's a fifty-fifty that a woman would wear a skirt, since a skirted business suit is common in offices. If so, she'd not spread her legs so widely. I smell no perfume or cologne. Could be nothing; could be something. I tend to think that men are more likely not to wear one, especially when talking of a fancy woman who'd dine in such fine cafés. Women who care after themselves would dine in company and usually someone else handles such incautious bills... This guy is not gentle with his paper or his coffee mug. I hear the constant metallic taps emitting from his direction. Besides, men are more likely to accept having to lunch alone to begin with. Again, all clues to favor probability but could be *so* wrong."

"Amazing flow of logic! I'd never think of it in that way."

"In regards to wiggling ears, I wanted to give you a hasty example of perception. Our mind is pretty exceptional in what we experience. I can't imagine what it would feel like wiggling my ears or, for instance, a tail, but say I did. It would feel natural to me, and I wouldn't understand how you couldn't. But, you don't miss it at all. Another example would be one's own mind. We have different senses, even more than the popularized five, but we can't 'feel' which exact neuron is powered at each moment.

"Look at other animals. Some could perceive things we can't and vice versa, such as infrared vision, echolocation, body taste receptors, infrasound, temperature-sensation, *tapetum lucidium*[8], and so on. Maybe we don't even know about the others. Sometimes I feel like I'm another species! I know that mice use their vibrissae–whiskers–similarly to a blind man using a cane. Except, their little "canes" can communicate with their brain. Speaking of canes, you didn't see where mine went, did you?"

---

[8] A reflective layer in the eyes of some animals, which gives better night vision.

"Oh, doctor, I tried to catch it, believe me. That's why it took me a while to get a hold of you. But, it flew quite a bit into the traffic and got scraped around further. I actually ran after you first then decided to bring you the stick while I help you up. But those dissimulators, which give other believers a bad reputation, surrounded you first."

"No matter. Only, I might get grief over it...And, I don't blame those church folks; I looked like a million bucks: dirty and worn-out—No wonder we call those singles!" They laughed. "Thanks for trying, young man."

"You make it sound like there's a huge age gap. Why, we're less than twenty years apart! If you think about it, you got so much accomplished in such a short time. It's cool. Continue, please. I'm interested. You stopped at the mice."

"Oh, my point is that generally we can't imagine accurately something we don't experience. It's hard to change our stubbornness and self-absorption. Unlike the common misconception about a dark screen magically filling an empty void in a blind person's mind, my brain does not concern itself with the sense altogether. Just as we cannot see the world's electric field, which some birds use for navigation, most blind people don't even realize just what that "seeing" is. The difference with me is that once I could, so I do feel a little bereft in comparison. Now I'm not aware of light waves relaying from object to object; I just know in my heart that it happens. On the other hand, do we really have enough information to state with great confidence that you and I saw the same shades to begin with? That's a problem with consciousness, which we are ethically scared to study. It's all in imagination. We live in our own virtual world but communicate to the outside through senses. I lost one and am, therefore, more locked internally. But it could be worse," Dr. Golggi flicked index finger up and down as if trying to get something to fly off. "Honestly, when I first learned as a kid about blindness and of Helen Keller, I covered my eyes with my hands and imagined how terrible it would to be. It really terrified me! A kid's worst nightmare: the total darkness. My fears manifested," Clyde chuckled to himself and swayed his head. "Of course, Helen had it bad, so I might be lucky. She's completely left out of the outside world with only her brain to speak. I have something to refer to. I try playing colors in my mind sometimes. Amazingly, I can sort of trace nine in my mind, though it's getting more difficult." They sat in silence for the time that seemed to yield space for the entire chorus of a national anthem.

"Only, I really miss reading," Dr. Golggi finally spoke. "I love learning. There's not that many audio books for scientific papers, and one can go through only so much fiction! I'll listen sometimes to podcasts and Discovery- type channels. Otherwise, I'm really deprived of learning, in general, even though that's what creates character. As far as Braille, I believe it's like raising the white flag; to me, it means finally surrendering to my affliction. I won't even mention hobbies, work, family...Truthfully, the operating room *was* my hobby, and I enjoyed meeting people, learned a lot about my patients. I wish I could continue sending them hand-written cards..."

"You must feel like no one understands."

"I think a lot of people feel that way," he smirked. "It doesn't come with a condition; it's the way it is. But enough about me, tell me about *your* life. I recall that med school was the most stressful time for me. Personally, I was relieved to finally work on my own."

"Well... I have Step II CK[9] coming up next week. "

"Ah, the big test! So, why are you letting me waste your time?"

"Nah,'t's alright. I'm relaxing, you know. Don't worry; I'm ready! Speaking, in all the papers I read about you, they don't mention what made you need the glass eyes. If I may ask, how did the accident happen?"

Dr. Golggi sat relaxed with his head tilted back, "I smell the rain. We better leave before we get stuck in the weather." And with that, the metal legs of his chair scraped the cement and stood up.

Cory followed, then tilted toward Clyde's ear and whispered, "By the way, the guy just wiggled his ears." Then he said in normal voice, "Funny, it doesn't look like it will rain. Want me to walk you home, Dr. Golggi?"

***

A while passed until the clouds filled, allowing enough time to get home. Things at home weren't any less mysterious. Particularly, Clyde owned a quiet get-away room on the upper floor of a medium house. The room was used in the past as a medical relaxation room or an office for contemplation on

---

9(Step II Clinical Knowledge): The second of three rounds of a medical student's board exams.

large cases that didn't get solved immediately. Once an organized and cozy little place—filled with scientific journals, arm chairs, body models and atlases, a whiteboard, a desk, and a portrait—the area transformed into mystery. Even when it served as Dr. Golggi's private office, he usually granted an invitation by swinging the doors open. Verily in present, those doors were routinely locked, and Clyde used it when he didn't want to chat.

Hanging the freckled coat to dry, he picked up a bag off a front door's low hook and traced the familiar choreography toward the office. Upon locked door, he took out letters addressed directly to him, which the postwoman agreed to drop in the slot. Dr. Golggi designed a system for catching place a bag on the slot to catch the mail, especially after he realized the incoming quantity. The mailwoman placed the others into the regular mailbox, to sort Clyde's from the rest.

The letters emitted a similar fume that in the past surrounded Dr. Golggi's old lab. Startled, he balked in action to take a sniff of the letters individually. One letter effused a distinct vapor of a ligneous, smoky lawn engulfing citrus then of olive fields caught among a faint whiff of vanilla beans. As light as it was, the scent bothered him, so he threw the letter on the desk before it slid off the edge. The rest of the letters were stuffed and locked in the side cabinet, where many more old letters resided. They were from fans, colleagues, admirers, past or unseen patients. They were letters that he would never get to see, as he avoided getting help in order to retain the long-established image of strength. Few were in Braille, but they became too difficult to read because they were glum remnants from his passion, even after he finally learned how to read some phrases. He anyways missed every other word, from time to time. His wife would sometimes read letters aloud when she caught them in the mail. He received emails as well, yet those he never opened due to ingrained "confidentiality" factor, so he didn't like asking anyone to read them. He just donated his computer to someone who could use it. One of his older patients, however, decided to approach this flawed communication differently. She experienced several instances of hallucinations, declined mental activity, and mild seizures at the time she originally visited Dr. Golggi, yet she was a professor of literature at a prestigious university. Other doctors dismissed her as a psychotic patient or some variant of age-induced delusional. Still, many didn't have an explanation and sent her on physical and emotional hunts. She heard that there was one doctor that could figure out a case that others missed, and they referred to Dr. Golggi, although he didn't initially seem fitting for this kind of a job. He was neither a neurologist nor a psychiatrist, but he could pinpoint nearly accurate diagnoses, which gave rise to the description of him as "Sherlock Holmes of the body." When Dr. Golggi heard of her history of type I diabetes and compared the clues to the physical appearance of her dropping face (unassociated with emotion) and a sudden onset of signs, he felt that she was abused by doctors. As her last resort, Dr. Golggi found a small but malignant tumor in her pancreatic cells, which induced a continuous release of immunity to attack healthy brain tissue and, more specifically, glutamic acid decarboxylase enzyme. He removed the long-hidden tumor, carefully suppressing the inflammation with corticosteroids. This was timely, so the continued decline ceased, leaving only minor damage. Her contact with him hinted that she was almost normal and adequate in logical thought, which was a surprising but pleasing thought in the time of trouble.

Her idea of contact came as a simple but thoughtful idea, and her most memorable words were, "You are the priest of modern medicine. When neither a doctor nor my dearest friend believed in me, you took the time to listen. You took care of me for days on end and followed beyond your duties to making sure I was fine. Even as I came to you in my pinnacle age, and realize that most insurance companies would rather invest into building my grave than waste on my breath, you prescribed the medicine of hope and the drink of uncrazy. Thank you for creating a funds program when all was impossible. You go beyond just your incredible gifted hands and obvious wit. I am much honoring my life to you. You're just the jewel! When I heard what happened, it devastated me. I'll gladly be your guide like you were mine if you find yourself battling all against one..."

The tape player then stopped no further and never played again; it was too solemn to hear sweet words about the passion to which he committed his educational life. The last thing he wanted was patients' pity. He was discouraged to hear that his office program of patient-helps-patient was discontinued after he left the clinic. He originally created a helpline to relieve the financially deprived families by having those that could 'sponsor' the ones in need, a fund to which he contributed a generous portion of his own check. Had Clyde not lost the things he found important, his outlook on this experience might be different. When it occurred like this, he envisioned the accident; upsetting memories create resistance against will...

The day of the accident began as an ordinary lab day: his extracurricular activity of which he dreamed to implement results. No part of research compared to the result because conclusion rewards through the visible improvement for humanity. He was close to uncovering the mysteries of his year-long study. However, something off about the atmosphere did grab feeling. It was quieter than normal, but something else so common was missing. The air smelled just like the chemicals Clyde Golggi used and nothing extra. There was no usual artificial spray mixing with other chemicals. Although at first, Dr. Golggi liked the masking of the occasionally toxic atmosphere, he decided then that the true smell of poison was better than the trap the good smells stir on the unwary nose. Raw feeling of lab was a great reminder of the reason why he was there; it inspired reality. The world seems to be filled with enough masks. That day reinforced his belief in this hunch.

Now, he was beginning to accept the outcome of life, but then that attitude was in its inception as only a relatively short time passed since the accident for healing of wounds to evolve. Still, some things prevented him from getting into his naturally positive outlook, and this emotional quicksand engulfed any chance of happiness.

For instance, the loss of Laila continuously scraped the healed mental wounds. Although that was not a physical loss, the pain overpowered other pains, even the death of Keepy that previous year. Keepy was one of the most loving, teddy bear-like, giant seeing-eye dogs serving Dr. Golggi after his vision entirely ceased. She proved to be better than a cane in all service. Despite the dog's old age when Clyde first got her, he insisted on this dog for she had a purpose. Subsiding over frontal lobe, his hunch predicted that the shelter was not the optimal life for this dog. Clyde knew that Keepy was treated according to the label of a worthless mutt. The shelter couldn't support all dogs they housed in the way those animals should be treated. Naturally, the owners' attention leaned toward giving the most care to the "useful" dogs and the ones that brought business. Immediately, he fell for her playfulness and spirit, but at home, her spirits exuded constant zealousness. Even Clyde felt a bit of a mood lift from her spirit. Right as he adjusted to the lifestyle, the dog left this tangible world, setting Clyde back in his progress until he stopped going out altogether.

Laila, on the other hand, was lost in her own presence. This loss created two, separate wells of mentality for them. They tried to unite through a common path, but Clyde gave up first on finding that familiar middle because he felt that he couldn't provide for his family the way he did in the past. He thought that he complicated their lives, which he previously worked to make better. Clyde overlooked Laila's approach to keep seeking that common pathway and egress this dilemma together. After all, Laila and Carley were supportive during the loss of Keepy and never felt themselves at loss of life but rather losing one they cared about. But what Clyde couldn't understand is why his model-like, modest wife stayed with him through this. Could the only gravity for this be her pity?

Once after babysitting, Carley asked where her old Precious Moments plushy was. She wanted to pass it over to the little girl she watched. She searched for it in the storage and throughout the house with exception to a few grown-up places. She never even considered that it could be stored in her dad's office. Within his reasoning, to tame something upsetting, Clyde held the doll up by the hips as if he's showing a child to the skies and drifted into hazy memories of Carley's toddler days: the times he held dear Carley up in that way. Eight years earlier, Carley was called the doll's twin, as everyone thought that this doll was custom made. Clyde traced the sewn features of the doll's head. He trained his memory to reveal the stored pictures of his daughter's young face. He did that for his wife when she spoke; he always saw her in the yellow, fitting gown that she wore when they met. Carley mimicked the beauty of her mom—but with her own distinct features. Unlike Laila's black waves reaching the lumbar and cut silhouettes, Carley's blonde locks twisted slightly past her soft shoulders to frame the delicate porcelain face. It was *his* blond hair that she carried. The same girl that used to look like a poster child was now scheduled for a real commercial. He longed to see her current appearance, to discovere whose facial features emerged. He missed the curves and creases of his girls' faces, revealing exuberance—as used to often form during weekend's outdoor play or the unwrapping of a small gift or the radiant cuddles celebrating accomplishments.

When Carley matured and entered middle grade, she enquired about what happened to Dad. At the time of the accident she was five and wouldn't have comprehended the situation, but at ten it seemed like a logical question. It was after dinner when the family enjoyed the warmth of the fireplace and rich cups of tea that she asked the dreaded question.

"I'll speak," Laila offered. "She should really learn from other human flaws to be protected as well as the truths of your accident." She turned to face her daughter and softened her delicately strong intonation, "Remember when Dad worked in the lab? I don't expect you to recall that, but he worked there his last two years in addition to clinic."

"I remember because he would change out of scrubs. He would go there after dinner and appear in a different outfit. I used to think he was a magician, not a physician."

"I know you used to call him 'Majy-dajy,' and we laughed because he had magical hands. Well, he worked there to solve some medical mysteries to further help all those nice people he worked so eagerly for.

"Then one day, someone who should have been working next door on a team project was absent. The two rooms had a common arch, so technically your dad could enter the other room by unlocking his own door. But rarely would you use another's door because everyone had their own keys.

"Your dad finished early, so he was packing to leave and still no sign of his coworker. In the hallway, your father, of course, had his goggles off... When, out of another hallway, his absent-minded colleague storms through, carrying a chemical on top of some food box. The glass slid off and splattered onto Dad's face. That's why he has those scars. There was also glass all over the place. The mess! Clyde, you cut yourself, right?.. Yeah, the glass somehow wondered into the house. I kept seeing little pieces on the floor.

"We weren't fast enough to rescue his eyes. It was a large quantity of acid. The guy "forgot" his own key, so he thought to use your father's door. I don't think he ever apologized. The next morning the man resigned, and we didn't hear from him. I guess he didn't want to be responsible."

"Wow," Carley shook her head in white shock then made a puzzled look, "I didn't hear that dad completed any research."

"He wasn't able to for obvious reasons. Some used his work to get credit after him. Most of what was left for them to do was type the conclusion and get a few confirming results. Clyde for some obscure reason wasn't included on the author's list, though. We let that go, legally-wise."■

***

They say it takes a surgeon to get past the humanity's skin-deep perspective. Yet, Clyde enjoyed even the inner view; he found more grace in the exposed organs than he ever saw outside, aside from external expression of two subjects: his wife and daughter. *Those* memories he missed. There, drifting free from the lost nightmare, alert thoughts floated about beautiful layers of the inside machinery: the same machinery that gained control of his consciousness. An avant-garde, tangled with the threads of light thought, aroused. The possibility for hazy wakefulness avalanched on itself when revelations seized awareness. Currently, no existing method could resume the half-wakeful state he worked, for the past forty minutes, to reach.

His weakened core muscles tried directing the roll of each vertebra to a sitting position, where he bowed his head while massaging his temples, then slowly protracted his upper body toward the farthest radius each palm could reach. Once he settled on the bed, the chilling thought returned and managed to radiate a frosty sensation from the fogged heart to its nearby, vital canals. He felt uneasy about confining his actions because of his will to lie—down, of course. However, where the cerebral actions occurred, things looked far from the other meaning of lie. He contemplated truth; it was just the wrong kind. His mind created the truth of problems when he failed to act on solutions, yet he once learned that each problem may have a multiple of positive outcomes. Enlightened about the lack of a desired plan, Dr. Golggi remembered the 'Pollyanna method,' which is what Carley calls positive reasoning. But his daughter originally acquired that outlook from Clyde himself! If he was to cycle through life now, this kind of consciously murky reality would not be of primary choice. Why, the idea was brilliant! Maybe he cannot formally research in the lab anywhere, maybe he can't see or treat patients, maybe he can't drive or go to the gym or enjoy accomplishments of his family, but he could do one thing. In fact, a variety of things are available that he could do, among which is theoretical research! Who needs the gym when the lanose carpet can support the simplest machine: his body? He's not limited in mobility; all he's naturally confined to is his dreams and memories, but they can go places to where human physical power was never able. He remembered Keepy; Dr. Golggi was still useful to the world as much as the loving canine was.

With that, the quest for theoretical thinking ignited. Ideas competed for attention, but a restless night drained Dr. Golggi. His best possible action called for sleep before life awakened. As he lay on the phrenic cradle, rumination about mental networks billowed. Neurons, glias, and all the accessory systems zigzagged signals inside his brain. And then, only a single idea lingered, as if dominating importance. He lightly considered the possibility of an astrocytes' role as a switch between dream and consciousness. What if there was a simple answer to the dream mystery? Yet, he was too tired to exult. His own dreams pressured to enter.

A soft buzz crescendoed, sending Clyde toward alertness...the phone. He hadn't encountered this alarm since his on-call days. Laila and Carley left to New York for Carley's commercial alone since Clyde refused to ruin his daughter's fun by trailing along. The weekend was about her. That was the one present he couldn't wrap for her, so he wrapped himself out of the picture and into his covers. To Laila, logic led to her decision on giving Clyde a quiet, allure-free house so that he can recover with rest, but Clyde's stubborn negativity didn't allow him to know that. Clyde groped the glassless surface of a clock's little hand, which pointed then slightly southeast. It couldn't be them; they perhaps were submerged in a fancy by now, after the day's wear.

The receiver felt cold but swiftly gained Dr. Golggi's warmth. "I'm up," he took a chance on his instinct.

"I wasn't able to sleep. I couldn't wait to tell you, Clyde, but I just found out that science is looking to merge the technology of cEYE[10] and the research on that brain-sensory connection. Remember hearing about those?"

"Yes, the Salk Institute's study years back. I thought about that. Why?"

"Well, now doctors pressed for research in how that idea could be implemented to the artificial eyes. They are actually making the eyes out of silicone-like material and then probing millions of tiny electronic cells or light-sensors that connect to the pathways that the study described. I want you to do it."

"How is Carley?"

"She's sleeping. I'm outside."

"Laila! That's dangerous! We can talk in the morning."

"I'm fine… I missed you. I was worried... And, I'm sorry if I awoke you, but I'm stopping by Johns Hopkins tomorrow on the way back. I wanted you to be aware."

"No, Laila. What about the finances? We have large bills to take care of. I'm not in practice anymore...What if it doesn't

---

[10] word created by author: the electronic eye.

work? It could just be another research bypassing the scientific method."

"That's why I'm stopping. Maybe if you're the guinea, they'll give us a break. Now, they will need time to develop the plans of production, machinery and such. I need your consent. I don't care; we need to do it! We'll find the finances if we have to. God's on our side."

***

"Sounds great so far. Could you go back to the middle, please?" Dr. Golggi kindly requested of me. "It makes me sound a little haughty."

"It does not. I told you, I'm not going to change it, because you deserve the credit. Trust me, from a point of view of someone who got to really know you, I think most would agree," I, the old English professor, opposed.

"I appreciate your genius efforts. I'm so glad to be on the other side of the table. I could never write as well as you have." I have to agree here with the doctor that I feel a little blush from the praise.

"Yes, I feel like I finally began repaying you for straightening my life! I said this on that tape, and I'll say it again: you're just the jewel!"

"I'm glad they wised up and made you the Dean. The word on the street is that you've by and large surpassed any previous dean in school's history." Indeed, I couldn't believe they'd let a 'lunatic' take charge of the students, but am I happy! I feel a special connection with each student and love guiding them to ease their college lives.

"Can you please sum up your life since the surgery, so I can work on it over the weekend. Then I'll give you a proofed copy to review. I want to have this ready for your speech."

"After the operation, I went on to formulate the dream theory but found some flaws, fixed those. As you could see, my procedure was a success thanks to the hard-working team of surgeons and the original scientists who made the eEye possible. I'm slowly improving day by day. Not fully functional yet, but what a progress! I have to soon start writing and reading on my own, though. I'm still learning how to operate with the eye nanotechnology. My brain is progressing on better interpretation, and my eyes should be optimally trained in half a year or so. I do feel like a robot sometimes—*I mean, really I have completely foreign eyes*!

"After that, I want to prepare and eventually resume my practice, possibly even add a field, maybe a fellowship. But I definitely need to do some housekeeping, so to speak, so that I won't feel out-of-practice."

"Got it! What about your partner and your finances?"

"Well, let me show you something here," he walked over to the drawer and took out a letter. "You can make a copy of it, if you'd like. But, better not include that at all as I don't want to involve the guy in this anymore so."

"It's in written record. You're legally allowed to disclose," I spoke but careful to recall the proper law code.

"He basically wrote that a psychic told him that something bad awaits him if he doesn't apologize. He blames me in some respects there, but I looked past that. I finally read my letters from patients and found it with the old pile. My wife pressed for the court to grant at least the money for the procedure from him."

"Didn't you tell me that he is in some country in Africa?"

"He is. It's part of his 'volunteering' option...if you understand my point."

"Any last closing words you want to include into your Nobel Prize speech?"

"Let me think about it...Hmm." He moved his head toward a corner in the ceiling and leaned back against the tall head of the armchair, looking thoughtful as if figuring all possibilities. Another characteristic I admire from him: He ruminates over actions before expressing his thoughts. He is those rare friends you meet in startling places.

Dr. Golggi finally spoke, "Aha! Yes, here's what you could write:

> *'I'm a victim who got a second chance to live life possibly more interesting than I imagined.' "*

....funny turn that life has taken, indeed!

Married to danger

Camilla's pinkish skin constricted around the eyes as her glare extended toward the adjacent wall. Her semi-hidden, aquamarine crystals traced Mark's clumsy flamingo act, observing the sock battle and clothes hunt. With each enhanced breath, her energy surfaced like that of an erupting volcano; except unlike the bursting, breathtaking peaks, Camilla was flushed with also disgust. The tension around her face wove wrinkles normally absent over her delicate skin between the eyebrows and around the nose. Yet her facial features, even with the center propagating an unflattering scrunch, with ease could mesmerize any man, especially as then her deep dimples have revealed. The early morning couldn't steal the sultry picture of the angel sitting on the cloud of sheets. Her crossed arms pressed her breasts toward the swan-mimicking neck. Never in her life has she experienced that level of hatred toward a human being. It was simply not her character, and this uncontrolled emotion further displaced her toward the treadmill of confusion and anger. She had a strong reason, and little in the world could compete with the brutality of her past.

Camilla didn't count on the swift reaction of her husband--who had been busy adjusting his dress shirt--to stop, with his collar clasped between hands, and give her a puzzled response to her unspoken words. The attention carved gelid flashes over her face, which absorbed the rosy-flesh and tightened her skin as if of the influence by an arctic gust. Automatically, Camilla's back stiffened while she faintly gasped, propagating uncontrolled horripilation through her body. Unsteady and flustered, she fought her way through the sheets but hurried into the bathroom to give an impression of some arisen emergency. Mark, bewildered, watching the door snap, paused before vocal reaction. "Is everything alright?" he hesitated to inquire.

"Ah...yes, I-I'm having a girl crisis," her voice pulsated the words with full thrust.

She focused on calming herself before she could *really* clean up. Then, she took her time in locked isolation before she joined for breakfast.

"Did my angel 'fix' everything?" Mark smirked as Camilla walked into the kitchen. She nodded.

"It's nice that you took a longer shower. I hope that it relaxed you a bit."

Glancing at an empty, pulp- streaked glass, she forced her words out through a blank expression, "I'm glad you had orange juice while waiting for me. Sorry about that."

Although she kept her composure, concentration was intangible amid preparation of eggs and pancakes. Her limbs felt dreary and clumsy, unlike her usual manner of grace and calmness. Thus, the eggs came out very choppy and uneven; charcoal blobs coated the pancakes. This meal was far below her usual consistent upkeeps. Even the coffee contained a sweet excess due to her slight hand tremor. She handed Mark the disastrous breakfast and watched for negative body language, but he just looked at the plate, smiled, then turning his glance to meet her eyes winked saying, "Thanks. A hungry man will eat a feathered bird," and he poked his knife into the egg as if eager to carve wounds into some fleshy masterpiece.

Camilla grimaced, in what resembled a sun-pestered face with outwardly curled lips, but quickly walked over to pour more coffee. She used that moment to stay out of sight so that she could *really* frown at him. His chewing made her sick, and she couldn't comprehend why someone that she would be ready to give up her life for could make her feel so heartless and such hatred: deep emotions that she generally despised. And her face didn't mask the anger well. Like an art critic in a museum, she was behind him slowly monitoring his actions by watching him from multiple directions. *Look at the way he is devouring his food,* she though, *it's completely unnatural. And the way his rakes for hands are grasping those piercing utensils, he's so careless. It's like he's fitting into a danger-driven montage of a movie. The way he's hunched over the plate like he's some beast about to jump his prey...* I *need to pray hard tonight after thinking these thoughts. Never have I wished harm on a human, but at this point, I have no care. I'm ashamed.*

The coffee cup in Camilla's hand emitted a chiming rhythm against the face of a small platter as she carried it to her husband. Mark regularly enjoyed an after-breakfast coffee, completing the classic ambience with the reading of newspaper's sports section. He sometimes skimmed through global news, so he would have a general sense of what the guys at work discussed, though generally his best source of news was direct gossip from Steve, Bob, and Miles; contrary to popular belief, men do converse--though using words stripped of feelings. Unlike on normal days, Camilla was glad this morning that Mark was engaged in the paper. At this point, she couldn't stand to look at or think of him, so she looked around for something to distract her mind while she forced herself to finish breakfast. She grabbed loose pages of a newspaper and began to search through the columns for something pleasant. It must have caught Mark by surprise because he broke silence, "It's not like you to read the paper. Is there something that you don't want me to see?" he chuckled as she met him with a tense stare. "Seriously. You're not acting like yourself today and yesterday evening, for that matter. Is something wrong?"

"Everything's fine. Promise." She hated lies most of all.

Camilla hoped to return to the state of a dream-driven world, so she concentrated on the paper once more, even through the laser-like burning of Mark's eyes onto her vitality. *Maybe there is a comedy strip in here somewhere*, she thought. A sharp thump brought Camilla back to the poor reality.

The Packers' game decisions upset Mark to the point of him slamming a fist, which of course spread vibrations across the red-oak table, rocking the section of news about recent convicts. Thoughts of local murders and Mark entwined her mind. She picked up her cup to finish the coffee but was so wound up that it spilled over the paper and table.

"Alright! I know something is bothering you. I don't want to put you on the spot, but are we expecting a baby? You are very jittery. Please tell me; I would be a lucky dad." This time he looked completely serious.

"No! No way. Well, not that I know off. I'll clean up everything. Mark, you don't worry about a thing. I actually have to leave afterward to do something, so this is an early good-bye."

"I thought you had today off?"

"Yes, off."

Before anything conclusive was reached, the phone rang, which was closest to Mark's habitual seat, but Camilla prevailed in reaching the phone, while paying the price for the rush as the granite counter bruised the side of her hand when she tripped from the run.

"Hold on. Let me walk to the next room. The reception is better. Now."

The man in the receiver spoke, "You were right. It was him."

"That's all. Thank you!"

"Girls, seriously, calm down! The whole cafe is giving us the looks," suggested the older redhead, through a tight banana-grin, then tilted the shoulder-length, deep auburn hair in an addicting giggle.

"Oh-ooh...let us *enjoy* ourselves. Not everyone has the luxurious marriage like Miss Camilla, so we need to get our fun on sometimes," excused the younger, with lengthy strands of melted red-copper.

Kelly, trend-setter of the gang, leaned in her seat to a position that best displayed her natural curves under a perked v-neck. As she used her palms to support her blonde bob, she calmly entered into the conversation, "Boy, do I have the juice for ya...I happen to know something that questions the longevity of our lovebirds' stability."

"Don't drag this out!"

"Yeah, let's hear it. Full blast."

"Well this might be confidential, but Mark did something awful in the past," Kelly continued.

"No way! Not to our dear Camilla," gasped Jane, the older red-head.

"If he cheated on her, there's no grace for any of us. He's in the dunks. Come to think of it, for us there might be a fighting chance, if he's a player like that. Nah...he's picky. Well, *I* have a chance; can't speak for you girls..." the other red-head raved.

"No-no-no-no. Nothing like that. Worse. Way worse!" Kelly interrupted Riley's blabber.

"What could be worse than a cheating husband?"

"A killer husband!" Riley chimed in.

"That's right! Besides, what husband is not a cheater, technically speaking." That statement widened silent Tina's make-up-heavy eyes.

Riley leaned over toward Jane, "She meant killer looks, right?"

Tina finally expressed her shock, "Wait, back up. What did you just say? Sweet little, hot Mark is what?"

"...A murderer. You heard it right."

"Whoa! Let's think about this. You mean Camilla is in danger?" Jane lamented.

"I wouldn't go quite that far. Maybe...now that she knows..."

"What's your source?" Kelly grilled.

"A pretty reliable one. Camilla phoned my husband last evening. She was in terror. She started accusing Mark, but as it turns out, it's true!"

"Accusing him of what? I still don't understand," poor Tina was pushed off the conversation. Her raw umber tresses glinted gold in the lighting of the cafe.

"He has on record what we call a homicidal action. And it touches freakishly close to Camilla."

"How many other women were killed?"

"Tina! Does the number matter? One is one too many," Riley criticized.

"I just wanted to know the depths of his depravity ," Tina concealed her upper lip with her lower.

"Maybe I better begin with everything that I know. And, don't jump to conclusions until I give you the whole story. Sometimes I think you girls are like teenagers. Gees!" They laughed to an abrupt silence. She took a large gulp of her marmalade tea as if it was the last she'd taste in a while, "Okay, do you girls know anything of Camilla's past?"

"Don't get mysterious on us. I didn't know her before Mark. Same probably with you, girls," and with raised shoulders, Riley spread her attention between the remaining ladies.

"Was she involved in something illegal?" Jane wondered.

Kelly shook her head, "Just listen. I guess her pre-Mark status would be a good place to start. I can't believe that none of you heard that she had a child!" Kelly knew that throughout this conversation the girls' faces would undulate between relaxed zombie and horror victim expressions. "I know it's a shocker to start with, but that's the beginning of all relevant beginnings. And no, she didn't have an abortion. She had the child and raised him well, until he turned fourteen..." She couldn't resist sneaking another sip of her tea. "That year something happened, and three years later she moved from Boston to our foggy San Fran and met Mark--alone."

"Ah, that means that she had the baby...let's see...when she was sixteen!"

"All this time she hid this important 'little' fact from everyone."

"And I thought that she was a *classy* slut!"

Kelly shot them a disapproving look. "Some knew. Anyway, it's all justified. Before you start getting upset, you should know that she was forced into the pregnancy. I mean, it wasn't voluntary. It wasn't even by a teen. In fact, torture is more like it, since, I hear, it was someone from her family." Amazingly, the girls' expressions didn't relax from the tense contortions, and guilt seeped through their make-up. "She had more than her fair-share of life's harshness. I think now is her bright, redeeming period...Or was."

Reluctant to say anything, Tina finally drifted into a burning question, "So...what happened to the child, do you know?"

"Oh, he was killed. So she moved here to restart her life because she almost didn't make it. But get this, she now knows who it was..."

The girls inhaled, "Hha"--then exhaled the rest--"...no-oo!"

"...Mark! And neither of them knew of the 'coincidence.'"

Camilla hastily raided the house for some emergency defense tools, but most of the silverware was left last weekend at Mark's parents' house where the young couple prepared a surprise anniversary feast for them, and certainly most utensils were left there, while they came back with only a small set of forks and spoons. Until the next visit to his parents, all that was left was a dull butter knife from this morning, and even within her vehement emotions, she didn't have the heart for torturing him. She was relieved that there were no sharp knives around the house as she didn't want to ruin her best sets. Even in anger, she couldn't imagine herself harming a breathing object. She impulsively headed for the cellar where an over-sized, iconic shield was stored. The crest was some ancestral treasure that her grandma repeatedly reminded her to care for when Camilla was a little girl. It was crafted by her grandma's grandfather and was a unique, artistic creation. Using a nearby white, leather glove, Camilla dusted the convex of rusty brass, which uncovered an intricate mosaic of battle fields and a family watching over strong warriors. She coughed a little, then tried picking up the shield, but unfortunately it was too heavy for her trim but tall stature. She was unable to even shift it off the floor; it must have weighted at least two hundred pounds since she is unexpectedly strong and able to lift couches and other furniture during cleaning, but this was the first time a piece has exceeded her strength. Then, she remembered that her husband had a medical kit brought from his work. Mark was a senior manager in surgical products and owned an office and a share of the company. His sales team was productive at achieving a large profit. He always emphasized the importance of his team for the society because his engineers made better life possible. And deeply, Camille could relate to his medical enthusiasm because they met in her own medical niche as the orthopedic physician's assistant; she loved working with patients. Sprinting to his home office, she found a tray that contained the largest jamshidi[11] and placed the sharp needle into the kitchen cabinet to better access it later. She needed a tool ready for tonight when her discovered information is revealed. In her line of work, she certainly knew how to use one the right way, but she'd never guessed that her training would be handy for wrongdoing. Yet the instant the jamshidi was safely hidden, she heard footsteps at the front door. Her heart skipped a beat then quickened in rebound, distributing fear messages within her mind, once she realized the severity of the presenting situation. Time-bound, she regretted that her limbs weakened in response. He wasn't supposed to come back so early. Fearing his response, she

---

[11] A surgical instrument--with a long, hollow tube (and inner cone-shaped tip) at one end and a T-handle at the other-- used for piercing the skin to obtain bone-marrow and in minimally-invasive spine surgery.

began to doubt her decision to mention anything and started to feel lightheaded. In reality, she didn't want him to know what she knew; she was one step ahead, but at the same time that head-start was leading toward a sinkhole. Loud bangs deafened the quiet hall; he must have forgotten his key. Mark could easily direct his aggression toward her; he hasn't yet, but he has those cards at hand. The door presented a mirage of depth. Camilla slowly opened it and felt a push as the door slammed into her.

"Thank goodness you answered! I walked around the house twice and wasn't sure whether to go get help." Kelly practically stampeded over the front door and was unwrapping her scarf on the go. Politely rubbing boots over the rug, Kelly leaned into a hug.

Camilla rotated and extended a free hand toward the couch, "Sit down, Kelly."

"My husband told me everything as far as he knew yesterday. What are you going to do?"

"It's hard to believe that my emotions can shift one-eighty so fast for the one that I dearly loved. I don't know," she glared at the grand rug, "I can't forgive someone who killed my child—even as I was ready to give up my life for that man. Funny, two people that I love and harm comes between." She apposed her lids in a pensive wag of her head.

"Hypothetically speaking, what if he truly changed and devoted his life to make up for the sin? Remember we saw that woman on TV befriend the killer of her daughter and forgive the stranger in court? I know you live by the Bible, so I'm asking. What's your take on it now?"

"Before, I thought that woman had the best qualities in her heart and mind and genuinely went against her angers to live by God's word. But isn't that deranged? The Bible commands to forgive for any sin as God would for our worst doings, and I'm not against that. When people ask for forgiveness, I'm willing to move on, but where have you seen a true, cold murderer wanting forgiveness? Most of them have a psychopathic identity. They know not what remorse is! If no one's asking forgiveness, why wave a cake past the dieter? I'm not doing anything wrong by not forgetting the murder. It was my life and light taken away."

"I didn't expect you to respond this way. But what you said is well thought out and justified. But what if Mark is not a psychopath?"

"I can't even look at him anymore. I have to ask for divorce even as I feel love for him."

"Aren't you afraid of his capabilities after you tell him? Do you want me to have the police ready?" Kelly got up initiating a wrap to the visit and implying the need for action.

"I'll try it peacefully. Of course, I can't guarantee anything," she wobbled her head then gasped for a deep breath and, too, rose. Kelly noticed stains of plum defining the lower boarders of Camilla's long, black eyelashes and the whites of her eyes giving way to flush weaves webbing through her typically clear eyes.

"Would you like to stay at my house? Come on," Kelly tried to grab Camilla and bring her to safety, but again Camilla's surprising strength kept her fixed to the downy projections of the tall carpet.

"No, I need to get this done."

Camilla sat calmly as she watched the lock turn on the door knob. She intentionally dimmed the lights for upon his expected return, making her onyx locks blend with the duskiness but contrasting her flushed ecru skin. The beauty's voluminous lips didn't wait for him to speak. In fact, her inveigling voice startled him as, when she originally depicted this scenario, she hoped she would.

"I'd like a divorce, Mark. Tomorrow," she started sleekly and ended in a firm tone. People sense weakness; she had none.

"Is that a new way of greeting that I don't know about?"

"I mean it," she tensed with no remorse.

"May we at least have dinner out before you explain things," Marks voice deepened. "Forget it, I deserve a clarification now!"

"I don't need to explain things, but I will ask you this: Do you know who my child was?"

Mark never looked so confused, but briskly he diverted toward the kitchen. And, out of nowhere, Camilla decided to follow. Mark swung his hand when he was near the table strong enough to knock one chair to the floor. Then the other chair just slid, and she watched him squat to it.

She stood by the entrance. “Fabien Villanueva.” To her surprise, Mark lost the color in his cheeks, which made her wonder what to expect next. A strong feeling of disorientation overcame her as if she was lost in the woods with an expressionless bear—who can strike at any moment—in front of her. Zero chance for predictions. She headed toward the cabinet that housed the jamshidi. “I expect this to be done tomorrow.”

“Okay.” Did she hear that or imagine it? As he was getting up, she heard sirens in the background but couldn’t differentiate them from a dream, feeling as if out-of-body and weak. While watching him, she slid open the cabinet door, but some sharp object pieced skin before her hand reached the jamshidi. Camilla’s palm dripped ruby liquid to a small place on the floor, and her upper body followed the bloody trail.

“Why didn’t you tell her?” The man in the dark coat looked at Mark. Mark placed his beer back on the bar’s table, remembering the night that the police cars were driving him away from the house. It was the second worst time of his life, which he will carry to grave. He was crazy about Camilla and experienced genuine desire and admiration for her. But away his happiness went as if with a puff of gun smoke.

“How do you tell a woman you love to forgive her son’s death? It may *be* that my partner pushed me off-course during the pull of the trigger, but no good man can stand between the love of a woman and her child. Doesn’t matter if it’s an accident or not; it’s someone’s life, and I’m paying for it.”

The old DEA agent placed his hand over Mark and spoke, "Listen buddy, I don't know what I would have done in your shoes. How do you deal with it? It's a shame that the code of the DEA stays with us for life, and we can't break the silence. I couldn't leave my wife because of this job, but you...I saw the way you loved that woman more than life itself. It's abnormal for a guy to love one woman like that," and the man's elbow hit Mark.

"That's why I left that day. I couldn't stand causing innocent people harm like that. I don't expect her forgiveness as *I* haven't forgiven myself for that night's accident."

"To be fair, the boy was caught with the wrong group of people doing bad stuff. I'm not justifying the accident. I'm just pointing out the reality of the boy. She didn't know that, did she?"

"Camilla didn't know that her son was dealing drugs with the mafia. And she's not going to know. She probably had an idealized version of her son in her mind, and no one should ruin a good impression of a deceased love. Mother's often love their children past any evil drape."

"First you surrendered the field you loved; then you surrendered the woman you loved. I don't know you to be weak like that."

"I'm not weakening; I'm considering my actions and taking responsibility. Someone has to. My jerk partner wouldn't even twitch for the pulse of that kid. The nerve, pushing me like that in his direction and making me totally miss the target. I had it, man. Had been trained to have it nailed. Was my chance to get that *real* bastard, and Bicky took my chance away. He let that...that get away *and* the kid die! I never forgot. Gave me nightmares for years. I'm in a business to help people now. Helping doctors to help people."

"How did she figure it out?"

"Camilla? She's clever, man. I had his death circled on my old calendar and kept the same gun that she probably read about when it happened. I mean, it was quiet hush, hush then. She was told that the guy went to jail. Only our people knew—our agents, I mean. I guess once she found that she had her friend's tech-savvy husband also do some deep checking on me. Good thing that I got out of that jail in a week after that night the police took me away, at least once the Commissioner recognized me. Lucky me, though, to have such strong connections to the Chief and have the same guy as the head for thirty years; everything was squared away.

"But most importantly, I'm glad she didn't hurt herself when she fainted. I wouldn't be able to live with myself at all then. I can hardly now...Anyway, I can't be moping; I have a nice job. I was able to keep it after moving. That's a travel business, so perhaps she's lucky that she doesn't have to deal with this lifestyle. I wonder what she's up to. Man, I'd give it all up in a heartbeat for her and a kid from her. Wish her the best. That's all I want now."

"I still think you should have told her. You'd be out of this rut and possibly some guilt. You need some closure... Forgiveness, man..."

APPENDIX

This appendix is intended to point the reader into the right direction for analysis, so use it as a starting place. I am not including all of my intentions currently into this work but rather am revealing the most difficult concepts. Be sure that there is more, and have fun discovering! Here is the selected list:

The **early-childhood** work is included to demonstrate the title's progression. The pieces are light-hearted, elementary, and repetitive, as they're written by an EFL child (from my first to fifth years in America.) Some of the grammar, as fitted, was fixed in the meantime.

White Muliebrity: This piece is an exploration of several meanings of color white presented in a feminine tone. There is some use of grand, unique vocabulary to make the poem more stylistic. "White Muliebrity" was my first dive into mature poetry at age fifteen.

Fly on the Window: As one of the few intentionally not rhymed poems, this piece records my momentary observation. That fly was real and inspired me to verbally paint the scene despite my slight aversion toward insects.

Beautiful Something of Nothing: The intent here is that there is absolutely no intent besides the artistic development of a simple object. The lesson taken would be not to over-think or overlook matter. And, poetry can capture a wide range of subjects, including raw nature.

Star Pirate: This poem appears in the newly released sci-fi novel *Star Pirates* by Chris Berman and was written at the request of the author. Also, **Red Moon** was chosen for Berman's past novel of the same title.

Life: Written in my new style called <u>sequential strokes</u>, "Life" is another poem striped of a rhyme and just builds words for each consecutive sentence. The form powers the words, and it may be rhymed, depending on preference. This poem pleads me to parallel with "Adam; creates life..." so forth, and in the future, I may cave in.

Morning Run: As a jog, the poem progresses on track to the right (in one of its forms). This is an example of my (di)rectional form because it is read either down or to the right without losing much meaning and thus creating a separate poem.

Reflected Beauty: Takes advantage of my style called reflection, this poem tries to simultaneously rhyme two columns consisting of two separate poems that reflect on each other and have their separate, unique meanings. A third way to read this multi-poem is to combine and treat it as unison.

A couple of poems, such as **Ballet** or **Poly-eyed** and others, have a reversal of rhyme layout, if you noticed. Try to see what I mean: Where does the rhyme start? What words would combine to feed the rhymes? This kind rhyme scheme sometimes propels some poetry.

Phone Call: was written on a lighter note. I tried to not get stuck in one genre by at least sprinkling some humor to my work.

Several pieces, such as **Sabrina**, **Mamochka**, **Mind On Model**, **To My Mentors...**, were dedicated to special individuals in my life who help me to become a stronger person.

Colour Series: These, on the other had, do have rhymes; some just aren't easily apparent because I experimented away from the traditional schemes. Try to hunt to see if you can find them. I'm a fan of rhymes but love to experiment with novel styles. The title is spelled in the British way because that is how I originally learned it when I was still in Ukraine.

Stairwell: This piece assembles the whole collection, for that reason it was placed and written last: the destination of this book. It starts from the bottom up but could be read top-down.

Sects: This is my first journey into the fantasy-centered intension, specifically written for a sci-fi convention's (OASIS) poetry panel.

Note on author's poetry

"They come knocking at the gate; they come scattered with the billows of colossal mounts; as I invite them in, I have to direct, yet more come: my poems. Those are poems that come from the heart of universe and entwine the stories of our surroundings. I write with flavor of a modern classic as a tribute to the giants that precede me, yet I desire to present fresh styles for relighting forgotten interests. Playing with novel styles and rhymes is pleasurable to me.

My nation's notable authors initially ignited my interest for poetry when I was still back in Ukraine. During early school years as my class studied literature, our poets' crafting of language impelled the development of my first journal of rhymes. Since then, I matured into my style with my third language—English—and even established a few unique forms of poetry. The first form is reflection, which are two rhymed poems that reflect the meanings from each other to form also one coherent work. My audience can reflect over that one...Another is (di)rectional form, which is reversed to the previous style, as from one stems two separate poems: vertical and horizontal. Then, there's sequential strokes, where each phrase increases in word count. Aside from the format, I play with rhyme schemes, esthetics, even hidden rhymes. Of course, the possibility that I myself can inspire some young author propels my creations."

~Marina Sergeyeva (Marina Buryak)

About the Author

Marina received literally a second life, almost eight years after the loss of her father due to surgical complications. The thirty-three letters that she learned at an early age of ten months would be unusable in this new life in a foreign country. Despite the initial language challenge, her poetry drive did not cease across the seas. While still in Ukraine, the greats and honorable of her nation inspired her passion for words from the beginning, so she then kept a small, Ukrainian/Russian journal of poetry. Here, she was a dance major in a magnet high school. She enjoys and practices not only the many forms of art, but also she has passion for the academics, particularly medicine. Now an early graduate with biochemistry and math degrees, she awaits to continue her journey into the medical world. Although she lives on the second floor, her life continues only upstairs.

If you enjoyed this book, please post a review to your favorite on-line bookstore.

www.leopublishing.net

CPSIA information can be obtained at www.ICGtesting.com
Printed in the USA
LVOW100504111011

249977LV00001B/13/P